MANTLES

MANTLES
Encountering Brigid

words
Shauna Gilligan

images
Margo McNulty

ARLEN HOUSE

Mantles

is published in 2021 by

ARLEN HOUSE
42 Grange Abbey Road
Baldoyle
Dublin 13
Ireland
Phone: 00 353 86 8360236
arlenhouse@gmail.com
arlenhouse.ie

978–1–85132–281–7, *paperback*

Distributed internationally by
SYRACUSE UNIVERSITY PRESS
621 Skytop Road, Suite 110
Syracuse, NY 13244–5290
Phone: 315–443–5534
supress@syr.edu
syracuseuniversitypress.syr.edu

text © Shauna Gilligan, 2021
images © Margo McNulty, 2021

The moral right of the author has been reserved

Typesetting by Arlen House

Cover image by Margo McNulty
'Forgetting and Forgot'
80 x 80cm, oil on canvas

Contents

9	*Acknowledgements*
15	*Brideog*
18	The First Touch
19	*Mary*
21	Love/Child
22	*Rag Tree*
23	Pips in the Hand
26	*One*
27	One Foot After the Other
31	*Cloch na Súile*
32	Threshold
34	*Hands*
35	The Final Touch
37	*Feet*
38	Mother
40	*Offerings*
41	Threads
58	*Drum*
59	Kildare Well
60	All of This was Wild
72	*Cross*
73	What Remains: The Light that Shines from History
77	*Through*
78	Unfurled
81	*Shrine*
82	Notes
89	*Portal*
90	*About the Author*
90	*About the Artist*

To our mothers,
Brigids both

Acknowledgements

To those before us who have created and re-created Brigid in word and image.

Our funders: Creative Ireland, Kildare County Council, Roscommon County Council.

To those who brought Brigid and her artefacts to us: Sr Gabrielle Fox (Redemptoristine Nuns, Dublin), Frances Clarke and Bernie Metcalfe (National Library of Ireland), Clodagh Doyle (Keeper, Irish Folklife Division, National Museum of Ireland – Country Life, Mayo).

Thanks also to Tony Cunningham, Tim Durham, Amye Quigley and Kildare Readers Festival.

To Alan Hayes, our publisher, for everything.

Mantles

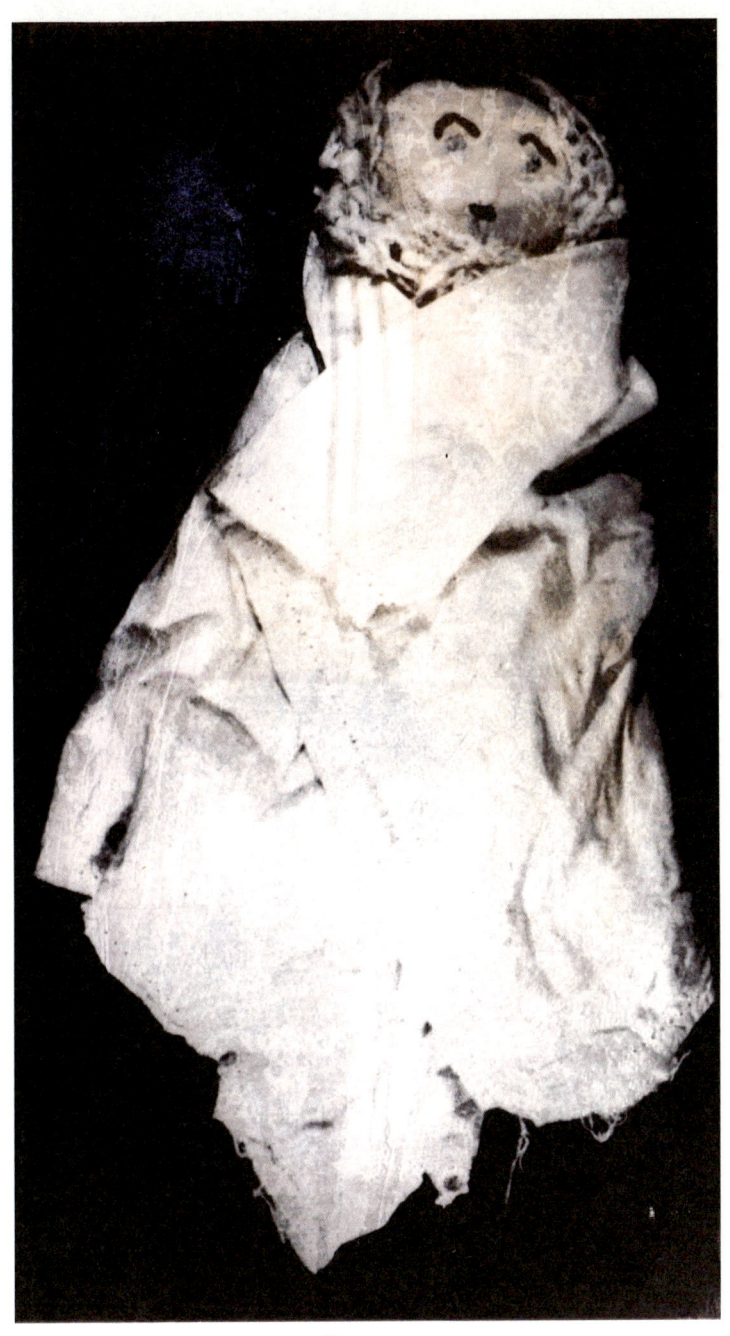

BRIDEOG
(photoetching, 59 x 31cm)

The First Touch

In the middle of a century, in the middle of a field, at dawn, a woman gives birth. She keeps her eyes and mouth open, swallowing as much light as possible. She wants to store brightness inside for when the dark times come.

A robin flies past, low enough for her to reach out and touch it. She watches how it works its wings, she sees it swoop down, then up and away. She remembers how it was said that when He was dying on the cross, the robin came and tried to pull the nails out of his hands and feet. While doing so, a drop of blood fell on his breast and that is why the robin has a red breast. This story puts a smile on her face.

Robins, like rabbits, bring luck.

The soles of her feet ache with the prick of dry grass, bleached by sun, flattened by bulls and cows. The animals move up and down the field. Some settle by the hedgerows, foraging for cocksfoot and brambles. The day is Saturday and the woman thinks about a song her grandmother sang for her. It was an old song that her grandmother heard when she herself was a child. You're born on a Monday for health, Tuesday for wealth, Wednesday the best of all, Thursday for losses, Friday for crosses. She pauses, shakes her head. Yes. They say Saturday is no good at all. But she, she reasons, she was born on a Saturday, and look at the goodness she now brings into the world!

The insistence of a bluebottle momentarily drowns out the hum of bees that is growing as the light pushes through the early morning. The air suddenly becomes fat with midges, thickening it like soup. Under them are piles of dried dung, and a little across from where the woman labours, where the cows low, fresh mounds sit, steaming and hot. The woman knows people close their nostrils when she is near; what pumps through the air and sticks to the skin, becomes them is *fear*. Of the new. Of the unknown. Of truth. Of light.

A slick line of sweat drips onto her forehead and she retches with the pain. The cattle low and butt heads. The flies swarm and settle, swarm and settle. She finishes retching, begins to calm herself. She breathes. In and out. In and out. They can't find her for she's already been found.

Shame is too kind a word for this and death not harsh enough. But up against shame there is love. And love, she believes, always finds a way through. She may be enslaved but she is loved. She has come to this field so that she may be hidden, so that the baby will be hers. She feels the baby push towards the light, and she moans, and she cries out at the wonder of it all. The pleasure beside the pain.

She reaches down to touch the baby who has arrived. Then she closes her eyes, feels the pulse of exhaustion. The baby's name comes. Brigid. She is strong. She is brave. She watches the baby roar, push her legs and arms out to fill the space around her, sees her feeling her way, making no shame out of the need for touch. To know where we are in the world, we must touch it. She wants to wrap her arms around the infant. Child is what mother is.

There are times when a name cannot be spoken or written; it can only be felt. The mother feels it in her guts and in the belly, and she sees it in the baby's body as it flails. She picks her up, and she suckles at her breast, eyes struggling to focus. As she feeds, the baby's heart pushes for connection, and perfect tiny fingers grasp the air. She is filled with hope.

The woman is thankful that she and her baby do not live in future times. For then, with golden roses on her feet – a beauty who makes all who encounter her weep – in her Blessed name, bodies like theirs will be – *hung, drawn, quartered, burned, drowned, tortured, denied, constrained, restrained, exposed, owned, used, mocked, mutilated, derided, covered* – and yes, all of this happened in a time that hangs like a cloud. All of this – and more – was done to flesh.

In this moment, the baby only knows the language of touch, but in time she will understand that her name is a shape that she becomes, and that becomes her. She will also come to know that with this name she has been believed. Darling child, whose life balances on the tip of what is no longer within sight. The mother whispers to her child, the baby girl, willing her to live – only as her self.

Darling love, forever go, without disguise.

And as you go – go, gently.

In the middle of a century – in the middle of inside and outside, at dawn, a woman gives birth to a baby. Before her is a door, a threshold that calls to her. She looks to her hands and sees they are holding pails of milk, the liquid which slops from side to side as she moves to the space where her life is already happening.

A backward dream is dreamt.

MARY

Love/Child

After touch comes sight.

The sun is bright on this summer day. Flowers come into focus: they dance in the light, warm breeze. Everything is hazy and at some point in her life she will want – desperately – to return to this moment when she can see, and not see. When things are misty and beauty coats everything.

The *illustrious daughter* sees this woman who envelopes her with her body. She is found in this embrace. She feels the strength of the woman's arms, looks into her eyes wide and blue and sharp. Her body shivers at the experience of being *seen*. She glances down at her belly button, suddenly fearful it has been ripped out of her, that she is no longer here, that in allowing herself to be seen like this she has become invisible. She hears the words the druid spoke to her father Dubhtach:

She'll shine like a sun among stars.

And as quickly as they come, these words leave her. She lets out a gurgle of pleasure, closes her eyes again. The woman laughs in response and places a warm wet kiss on her forehead.

What the baby's body feels is the transitions of worlds and beliefs into which she's been born. Feelings drag and pull at her soul, shapes of what is right and what is wrong blur and fade. She sees the life of this woman – her mother – spill before her and knows she will unbind her, return her to freedom.

She hears the word which guides her into full consciousness.

Love.

She hears this word, *love,* and begins her first act of creation. Her tiny fingers curl around her mother's finger, clutch the weary flesh.

I am.

You are.

Of, and from *Love.*

Rag Tree

Pips in the Hand

Fallen apples, ripe and waiting, surround her.

Any food her hand touches or her eye saw would multiply.

Dew still sits on the skin of the apple. She hears the snap in the brightening morning when she takes it from the tree, smiles at how perfectly it fits in her hand. She brings it to her lips, pushes down and up with her teeth, crunches through the red-sage-yellow skin into the crisp pale flesh that snaps. It is tart and juicy.

(*Years from now the Queen of Leinster will present to her a trinket with the tiny figure of a human at one end and at the other a silver apple*).

She's standing in a long garden, the grass lush with daisies peeping through, and she's being watched by the black cat that lives outside the place she calls home. He stares at her as she eats. Bite after bite he opens then closes his mouth, and when she reaches the core of the apple he meows loudly. He does not move.

In the now dull sunshine of the early morning she walks towards him. A gust of wind comes and she hears the leaves from the other trees crackle and fall.

And still the cat stays, statuesque, waiting.

Would you like some apple?

She holds out the fruit, watches his wet black nostrils twitch and his ears go back. He turns his face from her offering. She sits on the grass beside him and he, too, hunkers down, purring loudly. She feels the damp seep through the linen of her dress, but no matter, this autumn day will be fine and it will dry again. The light will come fully and then fade. The air is thick with promise, but this night it will become thin, thinner than the skin of this apple.

(*Years from now she will think, there is a reason this is the forbidden fruit*).

She returns to it, the apple, and nibbles around the edges, avoiding the pips, the core, the hard bits. What is it about these parts of the fruit that tells her not to eat them? Is it a fear that a tree will grow inside? Or is that what she desires? She holds the apple, at arms length, and looks at the colour. That paleness, that flesh which is not white nor yellow nor cream could belong to another fruit, surely, a fruit not hard but perhaps soft and forgiving. She brings it to her lips again and eats until there is nothing left but core with pips winking in a sun that pushes through the morning.

(*She remembers what a suitor said to her, just before she plucked out her eye, wanting to be done with beauty: That pure eye in your head is not much use to you if it doesn't look across a pillow at a husband!*)

Time moves.

Now she cups the fruit in her palms and a pip falls out. She brings it to her lips, glances down at the sleeping cat, still purring. A bird calls overhead, a shriek of warning. She looks up, sees a lone magpie. She closes her eyes, eats the pip, feels the crunch and the harsh bitter taste and swallows. A darkness washes over her. She opens her eyes to look at the tree that bore this fruit. At its trunk a magpie hops from foot to foot, dancing. The cat no longer purrs, just lets out heavy sighs of sleep. Feeling the weight of the core in her hand – though, of course, it weighs hardly anything – she stares and wonders if it is this magic that the magpie wants. She pulls out another pip, slides it into her mouth and swishes it around from side to side, her tongue graceless and awkward. Something is nagging at the back of her mind. She pushes herself up to standing.

(Years from now she will heal: a leper, a child without sight, a prankster of his tricks, the conception in a woman's womb so that she is restored to health and repentance without childbirth or its pangs).

And she sees it: the glint of the sword she will take as hers and give to the person who needs it more than her, more than her father, more than any man; the wealth that must be shared.

(Years from now she will despair at the injustice).

She throws the tiny string of core onto the grass and the magpie caws and flies high above it, circles around it, and then, cautiously, dives down and retrieves the reward. She keeps her hands cupped and then launches the last pip up into the air and watches it land and sink into the ground, and sprout, and grow, faster than her eyes can blink. What she wants is for the apples to never stop falling ripe from their white blooms, so that each hungry mouth is fed. Her desire edges towards the pip which is the sapling which is the tree which bears the fruit. She wills the tree like she willed the butter. Abundance, for the earth is nothing less than generous.

(Years from now, they will name her Queen of the South, Mary of the Gael).

When she closes her eyes she can hear the clouds move. She listens, then opens them, stares at her hands, sees the thin skin lined with so much of life. She feels the stories tucked deep inside her; etched better than a painting could capture, and more accurately than words. She hears the crackle of leaves underfoot. She stretches her hand out, reaching for the behind, the beyond.

ONE

ONE FOOT AFTER THE OTHER

The door on the threshold spells D-A-N-G-E-R as she turns the handle. Silently she moves from the inside to the outside. She hears the whisper in the air: *D-E-S-I-R-E*. She feels the glow growing in her breastbone, and she wants to name this feeling. She wants to name it, feel it emerge from the wet gap of her lips, cast that spell on herself.

She turns to her, her mother, and says, *I will take great care*. She gives her hand on it, shivers at the touch, knows that she will not return.

And then she is gone. She is consumed by the heat that draws her in, devoured by the land beneath her feet. As wide and as long as the cloak she wears, her love, her generosity grows and grows and grows.

Yes, she says to the king, the druid, the father, the master, the tormentor. Yes, my generosity knows no bounds. Yes, my love for all people cannot die. Yes, I am *Openhanded*.

The letters on the page and in the air twist and turn and slide until D-A-N-G-E-R becomes D-E-S-I-R-E.

Outside in the pale night sky at not yet eleven, smudges of bats appear. She fixes her gaze upwards, the soles of her feet trace the grass that flattens under her weight. The daisies bow to her, the velvet red poppy flowers brush her ankles, and she raises her hands to the sky and twirls. The moon smiles down and the bats circle round the tree tops, then change their position to an angle to catch an animal outside of her vision. The emptiness in her chest becomes filled with beauty that is around her.

She, *Brigit búadach*, must not stop.

One foot in front of the other. One foot in front of the other. Each step a difference. Every step towards that light. She is not beholden to anyone; she does not wish to be a beloved. She holds herself, balanced between the threshold of silence and sound. The wind whispers in the rushes as she approaches the river.

I am.

You are.

She is.

She has crossed the threshold and walks towards another. The thin lines shimmer in the faint light of dawn. This place invites her in. She has felt the heat in her palms, seen it vibrate in a certain light, known the power of want. What she does not know is the feel of freedom, so she promises herself to speak her truth and chose with whom she will walk this land.

She sees the end of the field bathed in a misty light. To walk it will take a long time. It might take a lifetime. It could take forever. The field she must walk. She looks behind and, though time has passed, it seems she has taken just a few steps for the edge of the field – this edge feels within touching distance. She holds her arms out, squeezes shut her eyes and asks, asks, asks ...

She speaks her truth.
She hears the disbelief.
She speaks her truth.
She places one word after the other.
She places one foot after the other.

She jumps back from the space beneath her which cracks open, the roots spreading, the trunk of the tree great. The oak whispers in the wind.
She speaks her truth.
She feels the incantation of the leaves ripple through her.
She opens out her arms, and waits for the leaves to spread, the birds to come.
She feels the *flagrant fire*.

Then she moves again: onward, outward, the width and breadth of her cloak twirling her through time and over land. It spreads, as her generosity grows: the more she gives, the more she becomes.
She remembers the future:
Cala lilies with white flowers and luminous green stalks surround the castle by the sea, in ruins.
Clover spreads over a well, stone aches for blessed touch.
A woman of mercy speaks of almost spent devotion on a deserted beach.
Gannets soar and dive over jagged rock.

She stands and feels the space. Everything is different from before – different and yet so much the same. The light has changed and the spring is coming. Everything is in motion;

confused, unsettled. She is neither here nor there. She is everywhere. Her skin still tastes of salt, her scalp is itchy with sand. Her hands touch first the green grass, then the rough bark of the tree which is now too wide for her to embrace.

Here, she whispers.

And she builds her church and waits for it to grow, multiply, blossom, the women delicate, beautiful, strong.

Cloch na Súile

Threshold

In the early morning the breeze is strong and the mist heavy like a mantle. It moves through her, like the spirits she feels every moment of every day.
What this field has not witnessed, yet:
Failure of crop.
Starvation.
Desperation.
Hope, lost.
Hope, found.
Love that does not save.

Pale buttermilk grasses move so easily with the breeze. Their thick dark green stalks are strong enough to keep them grounded, and not lift the bloom out of the earth altogether. They take on the shape of a crescent moon as they move with the air, never against it; if only men would move with life and budge from their ways of power and trade. Bodies for swords, infants for lineage. It will always be so, she thinks with just a light sigh, for there is nothing to be gained from ruminating on the habits of busy minds and idle hands. In the heat the nettle leaves droop and appear almost black; a drop of water will revive them and turn their gaze to the sun. Too much light is not what is needed either.

The cry of the seagulls overhead remind her she is near the coast of this island. The high-pitched buzz of the wasps, the scurry of the ants, the long legs of the spider – they all move with the air that she breathes, in search of what will nourish them, allow them to grow. She closes her eyes and feels the sun beating its way through the thin skin of her eyelids, the film of her eyes: dots, circles, life. The call of dogs – a moan, a whine, now getting louder, one out-calling the other – and she thinks of the hunt and the kill and the push for power.

She hears the words of the nineteenth nun: *Brigid, guard your fire, this is your night.*

Hands

The Final Touch

In the field, the air is crisp with frost; trails of silver decorate the edges of deep green leaves. The grass is frozen still. She turns to look back at time, how compressed it all appears now that life has passed; how wonderful those beings who graced your path with love and fury. As a woman she has learned to live in a world of paradoxes; she knows those rhythms, circuitous and slow. She's tried to show people the ways she's discovered, the paths she's walked, the mysteries she's encountered.

She thinks about *them*. Those who believe. Those hearts with their silent passion and silent prayers, how softly they bloom. How strong they hope.

She wonders if her energy is fathomless, her spirit everywhere? Is she the yellow of the buttercups, the sheen on a child's chin in the sun? What is she but another life? Still, she knows she will pass, has already, passed on the flame.

She closes her eyes and remembers the future:

The Abbess is raped.

The Order disappears.

Women are forbidden.

The body is unspeakable.

Brigid shivers, sees the flicker of a flame.

Brigid feels, the familiar touch of a cloak rendering her unseen.

Brigid senses the breaking apart, the falling back.

Into the water, inside the well: the wonder like a tremor in the womb, the flow pulsating – an eternal heartbeat.

FEET

Mother

Brigid, gem of our Emerald Isle.
Model,
Mother:

clothe us
    with garments of Charity and Salvation;
    Cincture, Beads and Cross;
    the Scapular we kiss –

shield us
    against earthly affections;
    deny our selves in
    the Guimp we pray –

remind us
    of the purity which should adorn
    Sisters, Brides and Spouses;
    the Veil we kiss –

separate us
        from the vanities of this world
        perpetually, everlastingly
        openhanded:

Intercessor
Mediatrix
Protectress.

OFFERINGS

Threads

Connecting
We are geological in our structure. There's bedrock laid down in our
early life and it never goes away ...
(Maggie O'Farrell)[1]

With this collaborative endeavour, *Mantles,* our intention stemmed from curiosity and a desire to explore the heritage and sense of place symbolising Brigid through archival artefacts and site visits – with the hope of rediscovering what she meant to us. The overall aim was to revisit through words and images new representations of Brigid as an archetype of the sacred feminine. The title came in a dream and with confusion. I had an image of my grandmother's lace head coverings: one cream, one black, both thick solid lace that covered her hair in church, thick, sturdy lace that I later used to push back my hair. I was, of course, thinking of a mantilla, the covering once used by women and girls in Catholic churches. But isn't a mantle a larger version of a mantilla? Is a mantle the same as a cloak? A shawl? Is a mantle used to cover or to reveal? How did the use of mantles and their colour, and shape, change over the centuries? Was I drawn to the mantle not as a mantle itself but to what it symbolises[2] – female divinity, mercy – *and* for what it represents – Brigid claiming her power, spreading her cloak over the plains of the Curragh? My ignorance and inability to distinguish between story, myth and historical fact gave me energy and pushed me towards exploring the archives. I was fuelled with the hope of knowledge, yet a voice kept asking: *what is behind this*? What is behind these words on the page, this beautiful, tranquil garden where Brigid is represented by a stunning statue? What is it that I cannot see? And if I cannot see the past – or past the past – how can I know it, how can I write about it?

Maggie O'Farrell's statement about the importance of place and where we are from set out my research map for *Mantles*; place and landscape seemed inherent to Brigid. Geographically the field trips took place across three main locations (though it did include many others). The research map started with the heart – Kildare: churches, wells – what is left of her – Dublin: relics, churches – and finished in Louth: her birthplace, wells. Parallel to exploring places associated with Brigid, I researched what was known about Brigid, or rather, what was recorded as having been known about her – biographies, hagiographies, life stories. For hours in the National Library of Ireland, I searched for clarity about mantles and cloaks. I poured over drawings of the clothing of the Brigidine Sisters.[3] Names of clothes that I didn't understand – not the word, not the function, not the shape – clothing that I couldn't imagine ever knowing how to use to cover or reveal myself. I wondered if donning these sacred clothes would be strangely freeing? For many women in the early and mid-twentieth century, entering a religious order was a way to claim a life other than that as a wife – although within religious orders, education and jobs were often dependent on the dowry they brought, and, in an echo of the Christian rite of marriage in the community, nuns were often referred to as

'Brides of Christ.' I thought about the enclosed orders, the silent orders, women who fought for social justice, helped the vulnerable and women who healed. I also remembered the harm, simmering on the surface like flotsam – or, perhaps more accurately, jetsam?

I considered words, clothes and multiple meanings and interpretations and how they change over time and place. I remembered the lace gloves, and version of veils that Madonna wore and how and why she wore them – for me, it reflected a deep connection to body and the feminine, a reclamation or redefinition of artefacts that had become too sacred to be sensual. I reflected on how the meaning of virgin in the mythological sense refers to being forever pregnant with possibilities, that – for all genders – it refers to a person who "has the courage to Be and the flexibility to be always Becoming,"[4] that, in the words of Esther Harding, she "does what she does ... because what she does is true."[5] And this truth is connected to the earth, and nature. Brigid is frequently described as being generous and in the fifth century, "generosity was the mark of the nobility and one who freely dispensed ale, to clients or overlords, was deemed to be *flaithiúlach*, which means both 'generous' and 'lordly' (from Irish *flaith* 'lord')."[6] Other words with seemingly singular meanings include *caille* meaning (at first) veil, then became incorporated into the word *Cailleach* meaning nun and almost simultaneously in secular mythology the word for an old hag.[7] How much of our understanding of the symbols and names that surround us has been limited? And isn't *Brigit/Brigid* herself the bridge between pagan and Christian, in both directions. It wasn't just her cloak (Brat Bhríde) or her mantle that I was searching for, it was also the Críos Bhríde (Brigid's belt or girdle), the Brídeog (the Brigid doll),[8] Clogg Brietta (Brigid's Bell), and the crosses.[9] Yet these artefacts are also associated with multiple histories and cultures, the gridle being "one of the earliest of garments"[10]; artefacts which are often only examined in the light of a Christian interpretation of history and the wearer. Everything suddenly seemed ambiguous. I wasn't sure what I was hoping to find of Brigid. Was it just what these items of clothes were used for, and symbolised? Was it something beneath the surface? I remembered reading that "searching for the perfect meaning is in fact a form of violence – it reduces and contains things by purporting to make them fully knowable, and becomes a way of owning them."[11] In searching for Brigid, trying to find her, was I trying to claim her? I needed to trust the process, and be open, without expectations, to encounters.

I'd always made a big deal about my birthday falling on Halloween, 31 October. What was the significance I thought I was applying to my birth-date? How much had I thought through the notion of having unseen power and being a girl, becoming a woman? And what about the hidden stories, desires, needs, and transformation of the women of Brigid not recounted in the texts stored in our national institutions? I recalled my impression of the Brigid of my childhood: a woman of strength and miracles who was also a nun of strict discipline and chastity. Yet wasn't every impression I had a reflection of what had been given to me? When engaging with her research for the seminal *The Serpent and The Goddess,* Mary Condren had asked why the stories she'd heard in her youth were "those of a sanitised and colonised woman, rather than the vibrant, generous defender of women's rights?"[12] My Brigid had always felt contradictory even to my child's mind to the extent that I equated chaste with strength, and believed the soul was more important than the body. What version of sacred feminine had I held close to me in the transition from girlhood to womanhood?

Another text I used to explore the importance of artefacts and art in representations of females in history was Margaret Mac Curtain's *Ariadne's Thread: Writing*

Women into Irish History. Referring to the cover image – a painting by Leo Whelan in which a woman is polishing silver and looking beyond the painter – Mac Curtain describes the role of art for the historian: "the artist supplies the clues for the historian and, like Leo Whelan's woman in the kitchen, invites the historian to look at a hidden thread."[13] It felt that the threads of Brigid had already been plucked at by historians, academics, writers, and claimed by the Catholic church. They were not necessarily hidden. My original starting point of curiosity and desire had expanded outward with each thread I pulled – a fact presented that didn't quite add up, a reference to a mantle that seemed to be too good to be true, an inference that appeared without foundation – and I came to realise that all of this reading, this research, these discoveries were not new knowledge. I wasn't hoping to find anything novel or claim to *know* about Brigid. I was not an archaeologist digging through mud for hidden treasures. Nor was I an historian gleaning gems from personal documents. What I was, what I am still – as I write this – is a woman scrubbing at the shine with a rough metal brush, trying to see what's behind the veneers of the polished silver, beneath the tarnish. I was pulling at the broken threads that connected with my lived and felt experience of the heritage of Brigid.

Reasonable Knowledge
I put aside mantles and veils and began to re-read the many versions of Brigid's life. I was dealing with a period of "the 'dawn of recorded history'"[14] and as such there are very few accounts of individuals from that period. Her earliest dateable Life (there are seven early medieval *Lives of Brigid*, the most extensive of any Irish saint),[15] that by Cogitosus, was not compiled until over a hundred years after her death. c. 650–80. I was mindful that much of what was written had agendas of painting Brigid –

Goddess/Saint/Woman – in a certain light. Many of the books devoted to her revolved around the shifting of power, itself a reflection of the times in which she lived and in the shift of politics – religious, sexual, social – with the cementation of Christianity in Ireland. I had to remind myself that I wasn't looking to find truth, or factual accuracy – scholars and historians had already done that[16] – but searching for how she was portrayed. Strangely, I thought, I was after what the *Lives* provide – accounts of her way of life rather than her life events. I hoped to *feel* Brigid through the narratives. But I asked myself again and again, "what can we reasonably know about Brigit?"[17]

The texts in which I encountered Brigid told different stories. Just as Mac Curtain had found Brigid to be "of dubious origin", her birth year varied from text to text. She was the daughter of a nobleman. She was the daughter of a slave-woman. She was both. She was raised by a Druid. She used her power and strength to heal and her generosity is frequently represented by the cloak that covers the land where she resided and presided, the Kildare of over thirty churches in 630AD, where "the mother-house of a vast army of Erin's daughters, who, by vows of religion, would consecrate their lives to the service of God (Cell of the Oak)".[18] The Calendar of Óengus, compiled circa 800 describes her and her nuns as "a shower of martyrs."[19] She was "a ladder to heaven for very many souls",[20] she was "Brigid the hospitable."[21] She was "a virgin, not alone in name, but in truth", "a pious maid".[22] In a children's book published in 2015 Brigid was described as "a wise and charitable woman who devoted her long life to the service of others."[23]

The symbols associated with her function as a goddess recur in the written stories told of her as a Christian saint; the images of milk, fire, sun, serpents are common in stories of St Brigit, while the themes of compassion, generosity, hospitality, spinning, weaving, smith work, healing, and agriculture run throughout her various *Lives*. Brigid, it seems, becomes these stories, themselves acts of appropriation. Further more, her sacred objects, her mantle, hair, and holy wells "were taken over into her Christian devotional forms."[24] The visual depiction of her life appeared to be aligned with the descriptions of her life. Many images in early twentieth century Christian biographies depicted her as a still, robed figure, gazing, or contemplating; she is often surrounded by animals – birds, small sheep, rather than wild wolves – or flowers – blooming and bright – and the tone is always soft though her expression serious.[25] In these images, she vacillates between the maiden and virgin archetypes. She is passive, not active, even though in the texts she reads like a woman who acted on the power she possessed and claimed. She certainly was contemplative but she was not passive. These images seem to serve as visual instructions for chasteness and devoutness. Analysing the visual portrayal of women from the 'old masters' to today's Instagram, Catherine McCormack notes that the "maiden archetype seems to say that being a woman means waiting to be taken by force (or force of circumstances) rather than acting on the strength of one's own desires."[26] Brigid is depicted as maiden and virgin though she clearly lived a life of active community and spiritual service as an ordained bishop. She was not waiting for anything. Brigid acted on the strength of her own desires and despite or because of her early circumstances (born of a slave mother) she was drawn to working with the vulnerable in society – lepers, enslaved women, the poor – practically and spiritually. Indeed, her identity "as spiritual mother of the Irish may have helped the emergence of Saint Patrick as spiritual father."[27] However, it was her prescribed legacy, shoehorned into woman-as-maiden, which experienced the violence of force and paved the way for women in Ireland. In 1152 the Synod of Kells put a stop to women – and Sadb, the then Abbess of Kildare – from having a bishop's jurisdictional authority (which began with Brigid). This followed on from the abduction and rape of Mór, Brigid's second successor, by the soldiers of Dermot MacMurrough in 1132, which, in the words of Condren, "symbolically and practically put an end to that lineage."[28]

Later artistic depictions and remembrances of Brigid focused on the duality she represented saddling pagan and Christian eras, often including one of the most common symbols associated with her – fire and flames. In my mind the heat of the flames reflect the colour of the Relic of her Mantle – deep, lush, red-wine – and provide a bridge between the artefacts and written stories I have encountered. We see Brigid's place setting in Judy Chicago's *The Dinner Party* (1979), where symbols of pagan and Christian Brigid emerged, the green of new growth and the orange of the flames becoming one in the shape of the female vulva.[29] I read stories that Brigid was baptised in milk, drank milk from a red-eared cow; as a baby her working (slave) mother often left her alone in the house and neighbours would see flames from the roof but every time they investigated, Brigid the baby was safe and there was no fire. I think about her strength and the heat of her generosity. This is what Chicago seems to capture: like her name, Brigid is fiery and on fire; she is body and she is light. In the frontpiece of Leatham's 1955 *The Story of St. Brigid of Ireland,* Eric Fraser[30] shows Brigid in celtic swirls with a fox at her feet, a duck in her arms, and holding what must be oak leaves but what look quite like large shamrocks. Brigid, complete with swirling hair, and the church are engulfed in powerful flames. There is so much movement and flux in this depiction that Brigid seems to be harnessing the wind and the sun – evoking the Goddess. Recently, some Irish artists have depicted her in a wine cloak, her cross as a weapon,[31] emerging from the green earth with fire above her and water below her,[32] as a well and with fire,[33] and in a dress of flames.[34] A commissioned sculpture of St Brigid in the Solas Bhríde Centre and Hermitages shows her in an active pose with her staff, pointing off stage right, a large celtic cross behind her.[35]

From the stories and pictures of Brigid, I delved into the accounts of the rituals so devoutly practiced on 31 January and 1 February by the wells and in homes.[36] Mid-twentieth-century, there was debate about who were the pure people, where the Real Ireland was, and accordingly, how Brigid should be celebrated in this representation: "We must go to the Irish speaking districts for those links with our ancient past, where they are enshrined in the language of the Gael in all their pristine freshness."[37] In Kildare in the 1930s, people would put a bit of hay at the door for St Brigid to wipe her feet passing by door on St Brigid's Eve.[38] People recited the words with which they were told to venerate Brigid,[39] words which in the twenty-first century are still used in Brigid Festivals.

Come in, Brigid.

We were asked to invite her in, as if we had no notion of our power as women, as represented by Brigid as Abbess, Brigid as healer.

Open your eyes and let in Brigid.

I imagined women's eyes squinting in the harsh morning sun, skin prickling with the cold, toes numb with chilblains. I saw children's mouths opened in anticipation of a cure for hunger. I felt men's hearts snapped in two so that they could no longer feel.

I have seen the bush with its pieces of rags.

Alongside calling Brigid, many customs involved going out on Brigid's Eve (31 January), visiting houses carrying Brídeogs in her name. These visits were conducted while making oneself invisible so that you become *other* – using cloths as veils. "In preparation for going out as *Brighideógs*, the children or any one else who is going, disguise themselves, so that no one can know them ... They mask their faces with pieces of cloth or curtains. Sometimes they make straw or rush hats to keep the veils on."[40] In this account from Mayo, the children themselves seem to become Brigid, being part of the land and nature (the straws, the rushes). The reward in the form of a few coins is, of course, an echo of that tradition of transition and a time of thresholds in October, when the veil between worlds is thin; recalling our pagan past, recalling Brigit before Brigid. I remember going around the houses saying, *Help the Halloween Party*. The communal aspect to these Christianised pagan traditions seems to me to be in sad contrast to the individualistic *Trick or Treat* society that we seem to live in now.

Yet looking back to that same 1970s childhood and further back, twenty years before, to when women were bound by church and state, institutions which worked together to create ideas and ideals of communities and ways of being. Examining one of the better known images used to promote Noel Browne's Mother and Child Scheme in the 1950s (a scheme which aimed to provide healthcare to mothers and infants),[41] I thought, women must have been driven mad trying to be the right mother, the correct wife. Using Brigid to convey sanctity and possibly in an attempt to alleviate the fears of the church about the proposed scheme, the picture, with a yellow backdrop, shows a woman with her arm around a smiling attentive infant; the image of Mary and Jesus. A St Brigid's Cross is visible on the wall behind where she sits. I imagine the smell of freshly baked brown bread, stories being told. I insert all the images and stories I grew up with in a country with tightly controlled narratives, in a country which choose – as part of the play for power between Kildare (Brigid) and Armagh (Patrick) – St Patrick as the national saint instead of St Brigid. Was Brigid too much – too female, too sacred, too dangerous – for a patriarchal church? Mother and child: the perfect maiden archetype, the perfect infant God. Mother and child: still controlled, still dependent. Mother and child: gaze and smile until you cannot feel your face. Images, after all, 'fix and immobilise our possible identities'.[42]

In the folklore archives I read accounts of mothers who collected an article of clothing for each member of her family, left it outside the house for Brigid's blessing on Brigid's Eve. I thought: every mother's knuckles are raw from washing, scrubbing, peeling, chopping, cutting. Every mother's heart broken from worry, shame, love, confusion, want. Every mother's desperate to protect. I read: "Many are the cures reported from the blest article; The clothes are carefully stored and kept, and worn should sickness be the lot of anyone of them throughout the year."[43] I thought: the food of the Goddesses – grain, honey, milk – is also the food consumed in most ritual binges.[44] The only instrument women had at their disposal in the middle ages was their bodies and so they flagellated them, encouraged and obliged to do so by the church. They wallowed in abjection, in their bodies, in ways that were self-sacrificial, a desperate attempt at leverage for some form of power, but ultimately it had the opposite effect – it resulted in their own death.[45] How many bodies, how many deaths have gone before me? How many women unable to be the virgin, the maidan, unable to feel their bodies, inhabit their bodies, have perished? How many of them in the name of Saints? Isn't it the case that each generation labours in the shadows of its predecessors?

The Brigid I'd encountered in the early texts had, by the mid-twentieth century, been replaced by a particular nationalistic version, one which was about control and obedience, not humanity, or nature. She appears pastoral rather than powerful; her connection to Brigit the Goddess seems to have all but disappeared. I returned to one of the earlier written texts with which I'd felt a connection. With the pen name, "Iona", we might assume it was written by a woman, most likely a nun; it touches on the sacred and on the feminine in the story of Brigid. A novice in dialogue with St Bláth about St. Brigid recounts how the call of the cuckoo told her she would find St Bláth in the garden by the herbs. Throughout this dialogue the women, in the way of Brigid, conduct their conversation by reading the signs and symbols around them: the call of a bird, the wind, the ground, the shift in temperature or atmosphere. Later, on an evening walk in the woods I heard the call of the nightingale. It stopped me in my tracks and I stood and listened, enthralled. I thought of Brigid and how she listened. This is something I am learning, still, like a child learning to speak, I am learning to listen. What, I asked myself, is the nightingale telling me? To listen carefully for beauty? I felt enveloped by the songbird and thought of a line in that same dialogue: "everywhere the fruits of her sowing and the sense of the protection of her holy *brat*."[46] Was it possible, I wondered, that I was experiencing what Brigid had once experienced as she listened to nature? Is the world that simple? Is time that narrow? Is the air that thin? Was what I was searching for linked to a memory – or a mix of memories – of what it was, what it is, to be a woman in this land? Or was I, in my body, feeling the divine as I gazed at the statues and crosses I kept from my Grandmother's house: St Teresa, Our Lady, St Brigid's Cross. Perhaps it was my experience of religion and the notion of female saints keeping me safe. I thought of the conclusion Mary Condren draws from the story of pre-Christian Macha, who was associated with the sun and who died giving birth after winning a challenge race: "care for the preservation of the earth and all her children must now become the precondition for, and the ultimate test, of any ethical system or knowledge of God."[47] *Care for the preservation of the earth and all her children.* Wasn't this what Brigid – Goddess/Saint/Woman – really stood for? Don't we recall this in our devotion to her in holy wells – aren't there at least fifteen wells dedicated specifically to Brigid in eleven counties?[48] Wasn't she the Mother Abbess of thirteen thousand nuns?[49] How close can you get to the earth – and beyond it – than through the water from and stone surrounding a well? How can one not be healed by the sound and the touch of water from the well? How can faith – in oneself, in the land, in the community – not be restored?

There's a story in the archives about a man in Donegal who refused to let the people onto his land to visit the St Brigid's Well. He believed his crops were failing and one moonlit night he went out to put up the fences that had been mysteriously knocked down only to find the well surrounded by hundreds of candles and then:

> He saw a beautiful maiden rising from the lake wearing a long white robe girded with a blue sash. She wore beautiful gems, she glided through the air like a swallow, and she stopped directly over the well. No doubt it was St Brigid.[50]

Visions. Forgiveness. Healing. Brigid gliding through the air like a swallow. Brigid not in her usual cloak, but in the robes usually associated with Our Lady. Images, memories come to my mind: high green grass with daisies and the sun hot on my head, the feeling of space as I run ahead of my mother and grandmother. Those two women: Brigids both, multiple crosses throughout their houses. The fingers and knuckles of their hands floury with baking; the wink of a wedding ring band tight in the summer heat; the steam off a cup of tea and that cup pressed to a forehead – the relief from yet another migraine. How often does the body express what cannot be voiced? I think of these as signs – womanhood, wifehood – and the journey they went on with their bodies, the bleeding, the churching, the covering, the silence. Most of all I think of the silence and how it might have felt to be silenced.

Rachel Kushner in her essay "The Hard Crowd" muses that "you reach a point where ... the 'material' ... gives testimony. It talks."[51] I asked myself, mid-way in the timeline of this project – as I did before the work began – what testimony do I hope for? What will the words that fall out of me say? What will Margo's images reveal? Where is Brigid? Everything feels at an impossible distance, but still, I *think* I might sense something of her beneath my feet. Mostly I worry now about how I can explain the feeling that she is near, that she is with me, as a guide to her own story. What I want is to feel is that devotion and awe that so many of the pamphlets and books I've studied describe. Although Brigid is depicted as a very particular type of light – chaste, virginal, devoted, benevolent, charitable – to me she still feels strong. A powerful woman. I want to find that light. And I'm sure it's somewhere in the dark. I follow the trail of the words, the language, the vocabulary – it leads me to the stories – that lead me to the histories – that lead me to the trail. I look, and look again.

Touch
A reference to a relic of the Mantle of Brigid of Ireland appeared in much of the literature I read.[52] It kept coming into my mind like a reminder of something that I shouldn't forget. I dreamed about it, though I had not yet seen it. The relic, the texts said, was kept in an enclosed monastery in Dublin. I sent off an email equivalent to a cold call. It felt like an impossible stab in the dark but within a day I had a response from the Prioress, Sr Gabrielle Fox: Yes! We do have a very small relic of St Brigid's mantle in our Monastery. You will be welcome to visit and view it.[53] I felt the wash of this generosity as a deep experience; the invitation seemed so like the Brigid I had encountered in the texts. Yet part of me felt a little afraid, as if the Relic of

the Mantle of Brigid of Ireland that I'd been invited to view, in person, might not be what I needed at all.

On my way to the Monastery of St. Alphonsus, I'm anxious and alert. I pass *Fuse*, which looks like some sort of dance place, and drive by a roundabout covered in pale pink and purple tulips and wild grass. I stop in a long line of traffic; to my left is a large sign that offers me a *Free Door* if I buy four doors. I think about the girls, and women who are told what they can and cannot be/do/think/see, and wonder how they would feel if they were gifted a *free* door. Step on through, they would be told, it's all free, there for your pleasure, your learning, your life. Your free door.

I park on the street and walk through the large, open gates, the well-kept garden towards the main building of the Monastery. In the Reception, I enjoy the stillness. I look at a display of photographs and sayings. On a small shelf sits handmade soaps, candles and rosary beads. I want touch them but remind myself we are in Pandemic times; touch is forbidden. A small sculpture catches my eye: "Finding my hidden heart". A woman formed in silver wire reaches out to a tree where, not in the roots or the trunk, but in the branches, sits a heart, also wrought out of thick silver wire. I shiver. Is this what I am doing with this project? Finding my hidden heart? The silence is interrupted by the sound of the post arriving: wheels of a van skidding to a halt; the snap of the letter box, the letters falling into the belly of the wire blue basket. Then I hear Sr Gabrielle's voice from behind the glass, apologising for keeping me waiting. I walk over to the hatch and she pushes the glass back; I thank her for inviting me. She looks at me with sharp, blue eyes – blue, I think, like the pale sky of spring – and to my surprise she quickly produces the Relic.

Here it is, she says, the tiny piece of Saint Brigid's Mantle.

I'd seen myself in a cool dark oratory or a tiny stone chapel waiting for the Relic to be brought out on a cushion, not this – not a bright cheery reception with the slant of sunlight and the sound of the morning call of the birds. A wave of Déjà vu comes over me. I see myself, here, with this relic, in a dream or in a memory that has already happened; I am remembering the future.

Sr Gabrielle pushes the Relic – encased in an oval-shaped gold case with a glass cover – towards me. What I see is not the white cloak – the dress of ancient nuns – nor is it the colour of a distinct order of Ireland.[54] I stare at the gold threading holding vibrant red-wine wool in place. It is thick and full and not unlike the wool on a sheep's back. Words come to me: *seeing the light*. It has power, Sr Gabrielle says as if reading my thoughts. I tell her I'm afraid to touch it. This is why – that power. I'm afraid. To touch. Of touch. With touch. She invites me to take some photographs. I use my mobile phone to distance myself from the tiny piece of Brigid's Mantle and snap, snap, snap.

Afterwards, I sit in my parked car in the early June heat. Sounds come through the open windows. In the distance, the cries of children in the school yard; the fading sound of a siren; and the insistent incantation of birds; a baby in a buggy calling *Ma, ma, ma*, pushed by a young woman in a dress littered with flowers. When I close my eyes I see the Relic in lights of gold. I draw the shape of it in my notebook. I think about the term relic, roll the word around in my mouth. There are primary relics – body parts – and secondary relics of personal effects or insignia (eg bells, belts, shoes), and also items that have come into contact with the primary or secondary relics such as pieces of cloth. My body feels it. I have been touched by a tiny piece of a relic, and it feels more than secondary.

One evening I spend hours scrolling on an internet site which sells relics, another trail that won't lead me to Brigid, but here I am, engrossed in the *Reliquary of Saint*[55] which includes a category "condition of item" even though each relic is, of course, used. These are wonderous and I can't stop looking. There are saints I have never heard of: Saint Albert, Saint Floribert, Saint Ludger. There is a Holy Relic of St. John G. Perboyre – Missionary in China/ XIXc and this is described as *in good condition, wear and tear according to age*. There is a link from the original site to Ebay. A statue of Brigid, advertised as a little taller than a soda can, offers healing in the form of a red-headed woman with red roses in her hair, holding a flame in one hand and a sword in another. Around her neck is a Celtic torc and on each arm is wrapped strands of leather. She wears a bustier that would not be out of place in a caricature of a milkmaid. Her expression is serious; this Brigid means business. There are relics in Italy, Arizona USA, Belgium, Netherlands, Spain, Greece. As once there were Goddesses and representations of the female flame, now sellers and buyers are everywhere. Everything has a price. Here there is no sign of Brigid "as a synonym for the old Goddesses of Europe"[56] with her cloak and her healing dew in a society that protects the Earth and helps the vulnerable. What I see in these images is power and strength and the colour of violence. Violence on women, violence self-inflicted in the form of bodily sacrifice. Violence and the red of blood spilled, not contained, not warming and life-giving. Violence echoing the times in which Brigid – all the Brigids – lived – and in which women continue to live.

DRUM

KILDARE WELL

All of This was Wild

> "The past is always influencing the present:
> the hidden stream flows on."[1]

I was conscious that "accounts of the journeys were formulated by hagiographers purely as a means of 'marking territory'"[2] yet I still thought about the journeys Brigid made around Ireland as recounted in the *Lives*. I considered these bodies of land and women, the need to secure and claim them for power. The earliest journey of Brigid was in utero away from her powerful father, supposedly to calm his jealous wife, and later as a young girl and fleeing the prospect of a particular marriage. It was a journey that ended in hiding. Some accounts have her with her mother, in others she is alone. As a girl, possibly about seven,[3] having fallen asleep listening to a sermon given by St Patrick, she had a vision: "a herd of white oxen among white crops ... spotted animals of different colours; and after these appeared black and darkly coloured cattle."[4] She then saw "sheep and swine, and lastly dogs and wolves worrying each other."[5] Yet at the start of her longer journey – in the foundation of her church – in all accounts I read Brigid was not alone. She was with seven other women – all in white robes – sent northwest by Bishop Maccaille with an introduction to Bishop Mel of Ardagh.[6] The veiling took place either in Croghan Hill, Offaly (according to Cogitosus) or in Ardagh, Longford (*Vita Prima*).[7] But what I want to find is how Brigid was on these journeys, setting down one foot in front of the other, sitting in a carriage, in a time of change and war? Casting off one ideology for another in the name of mercy? What visions did she have that she never spoke about? What dreams did she keep hidden, the images worrying away inside like a knot?

Brigid is present in placenames throughout Ireland, her name is commemorated in close to a hundred,[8] including the many Kilbrides around Leinster.[9] Could it be true that contemporaries of Brigid "renamed the landmarks, re-cast the topography of the island in order that she should be remembered"?[10] From the start of *Mantles* the water called. Wells, in the words of Nuala Ní Dhomhnaill, point "to the existence of a world beyond this one"[11] and, wells fit into the stories of Brigid using water to heal, tales of Brigid turning water into ale. In my readings I'd encountered poems and ballads devoted to Kildare and to Brigid; her "holy ground" of "The Plains of Sweet Kildare" has no equal in the world.[12] Even in pre-Christian times the whole area surrounding present-day Kildare was known as *Civitas Brigitae* (the City of Brigit).[13] And so, on a wet July day Margo and I set out to visit sites in Kildare hoping to encounter Brigid.

I want this trip to be successful. I feel a drive, an energy – and also a desperation. Driving to Kildare I wonder about how I might be limiting myself – what I can and what I can't see. I've filled a water bottle thinking I'll be thirsty. I've clad myself in talismans which hang around my neck, falling in various lengths down my torso: a tarnished silver scorpion from Colorado; a cross from Morocco; a crystal from 1980s Dublin. Why do I need safekeeping? Is it to hold onto myself? Is it to feel something of them, in the hope they will allow me to see, to feel, to *be*?

In Kildare town, St Brigid's Cathedral is closed due to Covid-19 restrictions but you can see through the iron gates, sense the coldness of the marble, feel how the Cathedral is without prayer, without singing, without sound. In a break from the summer showers, I place my hands on the surrounding walls with the moss, and shiver. In a café shop, coffee comes in a compostable paper cup, it is flat, white, and strong and brings me away from the woozy post-vaccine feeling. Margo and I chat about where we'll go next while we admire the decorated horseracing jerseys that fly high in the square. Symbols, I think, are everywhere. I think of movement and journeys, and how Brigid held ferociously onto her freedom. When we reach the cars, the rain pours. It's a few minutes drive to St Brigid's Garden Well, over the motorway and a few turns, the last of which fits just one car going one way. The wipers work hard; the sound is hypnotic. We pull in and the rain stops. The small miracle of the sun coming out happens and I run my fingers along the wall as I walk into the garden, the wet grass tickling my sandaled feet, the trees dripping from the downpour.

Behind the statue of Brigid – adorned with chrysanthemums, roses, peonies: white, pink, yellow – is a bush with white flowers that look like wild roses, heavy with rain water. A light wind blows the petals in flurries onto the grass. I smell the flowers, each one that is within reach but only catch the scent of fresh rain. I'm disappointed, a little flat, and I'm trying too hard – I can see that now – but when I look through the stone arches where the soft snort of a cow catches me my heart quickens. Tall meadow grass sways, three small dark birds fly high in the middle distance and wagtails parade behind the black cow with yellow tags on her ears. She locks eyes with me and twists her head at an awkward angle to lick herself. At the flick of her tail, flies rise upwards. She turns back to survey her field. I am in the heart of summer. I touch a petal that immediately falls, and then turn away and walk slowly towards the well. Prayers and petitions hang on the trees around the well. Rag trees. I stand still, survey them, feel the rise of tears. There are so many hopes, so much of life here.

> Glitzy white sandals dangle from a branch.
> (I shiver. Who lost their footing?)
> Babygros, hopeful and haunted sag.
> (So sopping wet they don't even move in the breeze).
> Born sleeping, a name, a picture.
> (My heat heaves; this place is heavy with leftover hearts).

The birdsong becomes overwhelming; I watch the wagtails flit and fly. There's a spot of warmth where I stand, right in the marsh among tall yellow buttercups and purple clover. I've brought nothing: no scarf, no sock, no thread, no piece of me that I can leave for Brigid to bless. I've come, as my grandmother would say, with my hands hanging. I look around, touch the leaves of some trees, and think again. My hands are hanging, but they are also open. I have brought *myself*, my full self, with all the losses I carry with me, hanging on a thread behind me, all the Brigids, generation after generation. Am I leaving something of *that* heritage here? Isn't presence in itself of worth and remembrance?

The water that flows in front of the statue of Brigid is cloudy and I want to describe it as misty, though I know that's not the right word. I stand there, thinking, and asking myself why *misty*? What is it that I'm trying to find? Everything that is hidden, of course, and I stare at the midges buzzing over the water, minute creatures swarming, circling. What do they leave or bring to this world within a world? What *meas* do we put on them? On ourselves?

Margo is elsewhere in the garden, taken by something, led by her camera towards a light, near a spot, close to another story. A woman and her daughter approach me – *we're both Brigids*, the woman says, by way of introduction. She asks if I know if *this* is the well which is just "for show", or if I think the other well, with the old Irish script, is the real one, because it's older and not signposted. I turn and look behind us at the well, the statue of Brigid with her flowers and her sheen. You don't feel her here, the woman says, holding a hand out to emphasise the point. I ask her where the real well is and she leans forward, and whispers that it's marked only in Irish, just near the Japanese Gardens. (In the back of my mind, I'm thinking, this is the same with the literature – there are two versions of the same story – two wells: one real, one for show – and yet there are so many wells and so many stories). We're going, she says, my daughter and I, it's only a short walk up the road. I nod knowing that Margo is in the middle of a sound recording and I can't interrupt her to tell her that we're not at the real well. I wish the women luck and stand and wait.

A while later Margo and I debate whether to walk to the other well but then the rain comes again and makes our decision for us. We get into the cars and drive to the Japanese Gardens. But I've convinced myself that the well we are looking for is off the side of the road near the Gardens, behind brambles, I am sure of it, I tell Margo, I can remember. We drive again. We do not find it. The picture in my head shifts. Maybe it's off a road off a road? We ask a woman out walking and she tells us there's a well on the way to Nurney but we must use Google Maps otherwise we won't find it. We ask a man, in Nurney, but he shakes his head, a sadness in his voice as he tells us that there's definitely no Brigid's Well around here. Kildare is the place, he said. Everything is in Kildare.

Who knows Brigid?

We are searching so slowly we create tailbacks. We pull in and let those folks in a rush overtake us. For once, time is not of the essence. Every hedge could hide this well, I think, possibilities are around us, we just have to spot them. Everything takes on the sheen of the unknown. Then I take a sudden left turn. The familiar becomes strange. I am reminded of getting lost in Colorado. Here I see tyres full of flowers, I notice the difference in upkeep of gardens, the largeness of some farmhouses, the neat compactness of others. Suncroft. Nurney. Kildare. We chase Brigid through the roads that bypass these places, the sun shining on my windscreen between the heavy downpours that only seem to come when we're in the car. We chase and we chase but we don't find her.

Who knows where Brigid is?

We make our way back to Kildare and drive straight into Solas Bhríde, the crunch of the tyres on gravel, the sun shining again now, the welcoming purple flowers. A Brigidine Sister opens the door before we've even reached it and asks us how she can help us. We tell her – and I feel the slide of inadequacy – that we are trying to find St Brigid's Well. I can help you, she says, I can certainly help you with that. When she asks us which well my heart leaps and we tell her we've already seen the one with the garden. I can help you with that also, she says. In the end we find the older well, so easily. It was there – right where the woman had said, right where we'd started but not looked properly – it *is* there – right off the road, at the back of the carpark of the National Stud, overlooked by the Japanese Gardens.

Here, the water is crystal. I drop a coin in, watch it sink, create circles of ripples, and I close my eyes in contemplation. I need new glasses. I cannot make out the words of the old Irish script though a date, 1953 is visible. This date, I later learn, marks the blessing of this well by the Parish Priest at Brallistown (or The Greallachs) on St

Brigid's Day 1953, the surrounds build by voluntary labour. The well is also shown on the 1837 Ordnance map.[14] So the facts appear as the well feels but does not look: significant. I think, Brigid never liked a fuss.

Later, at home, I do what I should have done before driving into the twisty country roads: I look up Brigid's Wells on the internet. Perhaps it was me being me – reverting to when I first embarked on research as a 19-year-old postgraduate squinting at microfilms of newspapers, searching for signs. Perhaps it was part of the process, literally finding my way. But it doesn't really matter. What seems to matter now are the experiences of others – also getting lost, missing that well, never finding it, some not finding their way to the Garden Well. The older well is referred to by one blogger as "Brigid's Wayside Well".[15] The blogger also includes a hand-drawn map and a photo-by-photo guide to finding it; they do not want others to miss it. A Saint Brigid's Trail tells me to download the PDF, follow the "mythical route" and "discover the legacy of St Brigid".[16]

Devotion and searching – that need to grasp – feel too closely knit together. Artist Sean Scully maintains that it's not good to want something too much, that "when you act desperately, things go away from you ... You have to allow something to come to you." He insists, in relation to artistic practice that "You never want to be out of your skin. You want to be in your body, in your work, and your work has to embody your ambition. You can't grasp, because that's ugly, ugly, ugly."[17] I remember the woman and her daughter at Brigid's Garden Well, and the expression on the woman's face that moved from disgust to sadness when she said that *this* – as she outstretched her hand – was *for show*. Is there, I wonder, an ugliness in commemorating devotion and displaying the sacred? Is the ugliness in having something for show, hiding away the essence of that place? Keeping the real Brigid hidden?

Or is it the two stories again: Brigit/Brigid? Or is this search all to do with the merging of the stories we have been told and the emergence of a new story, as yet raw and unclear?

In *Thin Places* Kerri Ní Dochartaigh explores how locations "can be associated with a particular warrior, hero or deity" while "places are tied to stories by threads that uncoil themselves back beyond known history."[18] Brigid, to my mind, is all of these – warrior, hero, deity – and more – feminist, leader, healer, carer, saint of many. She transmuted water into ale, broke bread, healing balm dropped from her fingers. It is said that Silaus, Donatus, Columbanus, Patrick and Brigid called the water they healed with *forespoken water* – which had the power to heal animals and humans, and bring fish to the boats in times of need.[19] I am drawn to the idea that the water was in conversation with Brigid – that there was communication, a communion, a whisper in the dark of the earliest dawn. I think of the thread of the relic and how it is dark red like blood when it appears. I want to hold onto that, the feeling of the thread, the wool, the connection through time, the energy that beats within. Ní Dochartaigh states that places "create ripples inside of us; the rise and they swell inside each of us in turn; how we experience place is completely unique to us alone."[20] In her book she talks about many places but they all spin back to Derry, and the multitudes of her lived experiences there. Yet there is something in this statement that speaks to me of my experience of Brigid – so far – not so much in the places where she is remembered and *seen* – but in the relics and physical representations of her. Not just the relic in the Dublin monastery that had such an impact on me but the St Brigid's crosses in my house – one in the kitchen made by my grandmother in the Irish Countrywoman's Association and two made by my children who were born into and have lived all their lives in Kildare. And again, not just *those* crosses, but in all the St Brigid's crosses in all the houses and in the reeds from which they were created.

The ripples of Brigid still move and shift and shape today.

A few months later Margo and I make another journey – to Brigid's birthplace. On a Monday morning in September I pull into St Brigid's Shrine empty car park in Faughart, County Louth. A mist has settled visibly on the horizon reminding me of how I'd had the urge to describe the well water in Kildare as misty. Here, in Louth, crows shriek and flit from the trees, cattle low loudly in the distance. There's an alarm to these animals' calls. There's a stickiness to the air. It feels too dry, like a downpour is needed. I've arrived here strangely: without any mishap, without losing my way. It seems customary for both or one of us to be delayed, or lost, on our field trips. Our confusion echoes that of the multiple portrayals and claims to Brigid; finding her is not straightforward.

I get out of the car. I take a slow breath of the air, my gaze directed not at the stations of the cross nor the Brigid statues but at the birds. Theirs is the only sound, the only movement. I supress an urge to sink to the ground with an overwhelming sense of gratitude. Instead, I get back into the car and think about where my feelings about Brigid has arrived. I think of snow and its solidity and temporality. I think of sand, and time, and I think of stories and the strength of lies. I think of what lies behind, and my desire to see beneath the tarnished silver version of Brigid that has been polished over the centuries.

I spot a woman following the stations of the cross, one-by-one, from the well, down past the church built in this century, to the large stones marked with the index of numbers which correspond to the Traditional Stations of St Brigid's Stream. I sit back and watch her. When she exits the gate to my left she turns and walks slowly across the tarmacadam to the long empty green field.

I want to let myself – my body – feel what there is to be felt, feel what it must feel. I get out of the car. I'm unnerved by the stillness in this place and let loneliness fill me. I stand with my eyes closed and when I open them I see the woman coming towards me. We comment on the weather and she tells me how the mist came down, very sudden, at about four o'clock yesterday evening. I tell her how peaceful it feels, even with the mist. We talk about Brigid and I ask her if she has Brigid in her name. She does. Kitty Brigid. She tells me that she's originally from Monaghan but she lives locally and comes here every morning. With the Covid, she says, people have stayed away from the Shrine, kept away from Brigid but – here she shakes her head in dismay – the other weekend the church, small as it is, had 51 people in it. Too much, we agree, it's too much and too many. I take a breath and look towards the field. All of this she says, waving her arm indicating the car park, all of this was wild, and the man who owns that field there donated this land for the car park. So that people can come from all over. I ask her about February and her face lights up as she describes the hundreds of people – and lots from the North, we're so near the North, she says – who come on pilgrimage and walk from the graveyard up on the hill down to the well and then to the shrine.

Margo arrives and I introduce her to Kitty who seems pleased to see another visitor to the Shrine. She tells us to watch her on You Tube – her at the entrance to the Shrine with a harpist – telling the online audience the stories of Brigid's Shrine I've just heard. This place, I think, feels like home to her, and she has taken it upon herself to welcome and educate people as they arrive. She heads off to finish her morning walk and have a cup of tea at home. Margo and I are left and it feels for a second like we're stranded but we quickly orientate ourselves and begin the slow walk, starting with the stones which are beautiful and on this warm morning are not cold to the touch at all. I place my head, or rather my forehead, onto the Head Stone, and hear Margo click her camera. It feels like I'm kissing the Blarney Stone. I am both moved and repulsed by these huge stones representing body parts: Head Stone, Eye Stone, Waist Stone, Knee Stone. I stop at the Hoof Stone where I should be reciting an Our Father, Hail Mary and Gloria and think of the Hell Fire Club in the Dublin Mountains. We continue, making our way past tiny colourful plastic flowers, miniature statues, a trickle of a stream, and new too-pristine statues of Brigid in various poses. We walk past the stations of the cross – donated by a local in the 1980s, Kitty told me. I realise then that we are doing it all backwards; you start at the well at the top of the hill and finish with these stations of the stream rather than what we are doing, but no matter, we keep on walking. I am reminded of Knock – though there are no shops – and a bit of habitual awe seeps into my heart.

Kitty had told me to pray to Oliver for work. Oliver is your man, Brigid is good too, but Oliver is your man. In the stained glass window of the small church, Brigid is flanked by Oliver Plunkett and St Patrick. On the steps up to her shrine, past the fountain funded by a man who was healed by the water from her well, statues of Plunkett and Patrick lead the way to her shrine where she, in statue form behind glass, sits along side the Irish flag and a myriad of crosses. I wonder about protection – the signs warning of theft and advising visitors not to leave valuables in their cars cannot be missed – and think about the remoteness of this hill. Like Brigid, we must be alert to all that is around us. I think of Kitty's reply when I asked her if she believed Brigid was born here, with a wry smile she said, well, that's what they say. I consider the wildness that the carpark covered, and the gentrification of Brigid, the sanitisation of the water – at this Brigid's well it comes out of a little hose, easy for the filling of holy water bottles, of course – and I wonder what we cannot see and why I still feel lonely.

We make our way to the graveyard, passing beautiful houses – again I think of Kildare, and the Irish countryside in general and how lovely houses and gardens are kept – and we climb higher, sharp turns, and winding roads. How much of the wild land of Brigid has been paved over so that she can be worshiped? Here there's another Brigid's well. Again there is a carpark – though of course not just for Brigid – and the cows grazing in the adjacent field are calm and quiet. The crows aren't cawing though the buzz of the insects fills the air. Brigid's well is almost hidden, and is deep and dark and something like emotion, something miraculous seeps through the thick air. We are at a height – on the Hill of Faughart – and I feel the smile form on my face before I realise that the sense of being alone has lifted.

CROSS

WHAT REMAINS:
THE LIGHT THAT SHINES FROM HISTORY
(BRIGID, 439–524)

The gold thread keeping the thick red wool in place appears in my dream. It snakes in from the bottom left and weaves itself around the red wool which grows and grows and grows. The thrum of my heart beats in my ears. Excitement expands through my body like a wave and I think of the ecstasy of saints. In my bed in a house in suburbia where a small window is open a sliver – in this warm June – I may be moving a leg, or an arm, extending myself out like an offering, wanting the ecstasy of my dream to pass into my waking – or night – life. The pattern of the cloak – not to be confused with the mantle – or the pattern of the mantle – not be confused with the cloak – is spread out, cloud-like, above me and I watch, in total awe, as the thread and the wool fly up to that pattern. The movement is magnetic. The white of the pattern and the blue lines marking stitches disappear behind the bold red, the gleaming gold. I feel myself floating upwards – I too am magnetic, I realise, and I hear my laughter, raw and real and mad. I become aware that the thread is part of the mantle; it is not holding it in place, in fact, each stitch is a stitch nearer to the Divine, each stitch brings the wearer closer to the sacred, to the feminine. I am awed. Then like Alice I am twirled right around, whizzing through time, dropping through my consciousness while the mantle shrinks back to a relic in a golden case, in a Monastery of light and serenity, and I am standing by my bed in a dark room staring at the light that shines from history.

In my waking sorrow is the strength of love.

In another time, with less restrictions, I would have travelled to Bruges, Belgium and to Lumiar, Portugal to find the physical pieces of Brigid. Instead, I still dream of her mantle expanding in my arms. I sit with the experience of the journeys to wells, the books and pamphlets I've read, the images I've seen, the people I've talked to and the stories I've heard. Rev J.A. Knowles tells us in the introduction to his biography of Brigid that if the children of "this favoured land ever forget their benefactress and patroness", the walls of the temples would crumble, the holy wells would go dry and the "fertile soil of the four provinces consecrated by her missionary footsteps would cease to yield their rich golden harvests."[1] What remains? What remains are the multitudes of Brigids echoing the myriads of myths and stories. I consider the name and the claim to the name of Brigid, and all its variants, the line of Brigids in my family, and how I've passed the name on to my daughter. Alice Curtayne, writing in mid-twentieth-century Kildare, claimed that people were missing the *singularity* of Brigid and now, almost a century later, I feel it is the *plurality* (or is it the pluralities) of Brigid that we need to see. Does it matter if we don't know where the certainty about Brigid begins, and ends? While "the sixth century loved her supremely",[2] why do we need to account "for the fascination exercised by Brigid?"[3] – surely we should be making the hidden Brigid visible?[4]

What we are able to see remains conditioned by the archetypes and visual language available to us but "when we change the way we see, the things we see also change."[5] Brigid chose life over death-by-marriage, life over death-by-child, life over death-by-wealth. Brigid decided what life would live in her body and what life her body would and would not live. What are our choices now? What do we and how do choose? How can I see anew what is shown to me of Brigid? Brigid, it feels to me, had so many homes she was homeless, so many churches she was churchless, is so many women to so many people that she is nobody. And yet. Her bones may be scattered across Europe and worshiped throughout the world, but the fire of her work, her legacy still lives on; it's just that the church has some catching-up, or catching-back-up in relation to female ordination; it's just that the state has some waking up to do; it's just that true equity and equality has yet to come.

After Brigid's death at eighty-eight, or eighty-five-or-six,[6] people "prayed to her for help in time of difficulty and danger. They called to her to calm storms and banish plagues".[7] Is it a coincidence that we are drawn to Brigid in this global pandemic, a time of such change to land, environment, climate, our whole way of life? Every time I encounter Brigid, there is flux. We see her "in the winds of change",[8] she is "about cultivating creativity in everyone,"[9] she's a woman who "brings a lot of life, a lot of light, a lot of meaning."[10] Could this liminal multitude be a harbinger of change? "Desire," Deborah Levy says in *Real Estate*, "is not always kind". When I was a child I wished I had no body. Without a body – this heavy trembling thing of burden and shame and fluids and needs, this thing that needed to be fed – my existence would be simple, light and free. I *desired* not to have a body. Now I think, if I were without a body would I be like Brigid? A generous light? Isn't that what she, too, desired? To be without the burden of body? Wasn't that what she was looking for? I ask myself, is her story that of a woman's pluck, a woman's lucky escape from bondage, a woman creating her own world within and despite the limitations she faced? Wasn't her life lived on the basis of freedom?

On a day in early autumn, I watch the insects, listen to the buzz of the flying ones – bees, wasps, working, working, working – and I think: *we are all killers*. I cannot walk across the grass without inflicting near death or death on something that is smaller than me. I am no Francis-of-Assisi. I am no Teresa-of-roses. I am no Brigid-of-Kildare. The sound of magpies calling becomes more frantic. I spot my cat cackling at them and think, when Brigid talked to birds she also listened. I am listening – but what am I hearing? Following her around the country has made me more aware of the choices we make, and decisions we do not take. I want to walk the paths where she walked. Brigid's Way on main roads, through housing estates, past fields. Brigid's presence remains. Seeing the relic of Brigid's mantle has opened something in me, like the edge of an envelope. It's still sticky, still stuck, but it's becoming undone, and opening slowly. Is it sacred? Is it feminine? I still see the fleece of the relic, the ancient weave of pre-Christian times. If I open my heart I can just about feel the heat of the flame, hear the crackle of the fire, know the healing of hands, and believe that I, too, am part of this female lineage that could not be destroyed.

THROUGH

Unfurled

Once upon a time there was a girl who was the harbinger of the girl with the cape with the hood, of the girl with red blood.

She heard her calling each morning when she woke. When she walked, and as she worked, she felt a shifting, like the wings of a butterfly. Her body was blooming, becoming a resting throne, a vessel, with abundance and flow. She knew that her burden of beauty was so heavy that she must shed it. She was obliged to cover every trace and thread of it.

On the day she abandoned the life foretold for her she said to her mother: *I will take great care*, and she gave her hand on it. Her mother embraced her, knowing the thread between them would never be broken. In those moments of touch what secrets passed between mother and daughter?

Little Brigid's benevolence unfurled like swirls of soft butter. Her generosity surpassed that of the trees; her happiness travelled in the wind to those she did not yet know.

She roamed, and listened to what the birds, the wild wolves and boars told her and she went to where the oak trees grew. She followed the land, with seven women, white-caped like her, and streamed across green landscapes. She carried lightly her heat, held her knowledge, glowing. She spread her cloak, and it grew in patches like the land. Her heart healed and hurt, hurt and healed.

Or perhaps, through another lens, as a woman, she was not bound by circumstance to Kildare. She travelled across the country – never rushing – and with each step she took, each rattle of the carriage, Kildare claimed a little more power and the thread connecting to her Louth thinned. She cured Ninnid, a saint-in-the-making, of speed and hurry. He learned to feel what was beneath his feet, to understand the bleats of the sheep, to heed the cry of the gulls when they were in-land. He followed Brigid as deliberately as the lambs. Once, a leper who refused to wash the sores of his brother in distress cried out: just now I feel sparks of fire settling on my shoulders. Witnesses saw Brigid's body ramrod-straight, her mouth a furnace of noise, her face red with fury. But Brigid also listened to the birds and their calls of plenty. The birds saw her as a sun amidst the stars, the vine among the trees, the dove among the birds who come to her when she called. Did they ask: Is it the pause and waiting that bring the wolves to her? Is it her acceptance of everything? Is it her open hands? Or, as centuries turned, did they wonder: What is a woman if she is not wife, mother, daughter? What is a woman if she is not body, vessel, nourishment?

When she crossed the threshold of time, she closed her eyes to feel the rain, to take in the warmth of the rays – in balance and fairness. In her intentions and deeds she was as much open-hearted as open-handed. The colours shift and shimmer and the vision is of a woman – who once managed between 11,00 and 15,000 nuns and was ordained a bishop – now silently reciting prayers, whispering mantras. Modest, meek, humble and chaste, as generous as the trees, Brigid was a panegyric, spoken about not in hushed tones but in voices which carried across the steps of the theatre, the rocks of the mountains, the hills on which sheep graze overlooking villages filled with expectant people. Waiting. Waiting for Brigid.

With age, the weight of her body gradually disappeared beneath the covering, the cloak, the mantle, the eyes cast downwards.

She became a symbol – not herself, nor her body, nor the grass upon which she once lay yearning for more. She was a vehicle – a ladder to heaven for very many – a hope through which people passed.

Then when she, her essence, breathed on this earth for the last time, her body was plundered:

severed
carried
kept
cherished
worshiped
lost
taken
presented
gifted
treasured

Across time, those who behold and those who hold feel her presence:
   In their bones, a burning.
   In their hair, a light wind.
   In their ear, a whisper of hope.

SHRINE

Notes

Threads

1. Maggie O'Farrell in interview with Elizabeth Day, *How To Fail*, Series 11, Episode 8, 14 July 2021.
2. Mary Condren (January 2021) discusses this in detail: *WATERtea with Mary Condren*, "Preparing to Celebrate the Festival of Brigid" https://www.youtube.com/watch?v=ZYEScCuQ9us [Accessed 17/08/2021]
3. Margo and I had been given permission to access the archives of the Brigidine Sisters in The Delany Archives in Carlow College. The archivist Bernie Deasy, after I exchanged emails and had a telephone discussion with her about the project, had kindly selected a number of artefacts that related to Brigid and mantles. Unfortunately due to Covid-19 restrictions it was not possible to visit the archive, and, as it was closed over the summer months, we were unable to gain access to the artefacts. I had always planned to research in the National Library of Ireland as well so plan b became plan a.
4. Marion Woodman, *The Pregnant Virgin: A Process of Psychological Transformation* (New York, Inner City Books, 1985), p. 78.
5. Esther Harding, quoted in Woodman, p. 76.
6. Angela Bourke *et al* (eds), *The Field Day Anthology of Irish Writing, Volume V: Irish Women's Writings and Traditions* (Cork, Cork University Press, 2002), p. 73.
7. Margaret Mac Curtain, *Ariadne's Thread: Writing Women into Irish History* (Galway, Arlen House, 2008), p. 104.
8. The Brídeog is a large doll or image often made of straw and clothed in white or in various colours according to the customs of the particular area and is carried from house to house by a group of people known as 'Lucht na Brídeoige'. The image is called the Brídeog but the name is also given to the actual rite of visitation. Seán Ó Duinn, *The Rites of Brigid: Goddess and Saint* (Dublin, Columba Press, 2005), p. 84. According to Ó Duinn, this was a custom mainly practiced in the south of the country (eg. Kerry) with the Threshold Rite on Brigid's Eve being more common in the north. From my research in the Schools' Collection (UCD National Folklore Collection), it would appear that some of these rituals also took place in Mayo and in Kildare. Clodagh Doyle, Keeper, Irish Folklife Division, National Museum of Ireland –

Country Life, Mayo confirmed in conversation with the authors (at Kildare Readers Festival, 2021) that the four-armed cross gained popularity mid twentieth century.
9 According to Ó Duinn, *ibid*, p. 121, there are seven types of crosses: 1. The four-armed or 'Swastika' type, 2. The three armed type, 3. The diamond or 'lozenge' type, 4. the interwoven type, 5. St Brigid's Bow, 6. St. Brigid's bare cross, 7. The Sheaf Cross. Crosses can be viewed in the Museum of Country Life, Mayo.
10 Walter J. Dilling, "Girdles: Their origin and development particularly with regards to their use as charms in medicine, marriage, and midwifery". Wellcome Collection 1913–1914. https://wellcomecollection.org/works/canvfd8p/items?canvas=10 [Accessed 17/08/2021]
11 Catherine McCormack, *Women in The Picture: Women, Art and the Power of Looking* (London: Icon Books, 2021), p. 206.
12 Mary Condren *The Serpent and The Goddess* (Dublin, New Island, 2002 [1989]), p. xviii.
13 Mac Curtain, *op cit*, p. 122.
14 Noel Kissane, *Saint Brigid of Kildare: Life, Legend and Cult* (Dublin, Four Courts Press/Open Air, 2017), p. 94.
15 *Ibid*, p. 73. Kissane also gives a clear account of the *Lives* and various biographies and hagiographies of Brigid in Chapter 3.
16 For example, see Chapter 1 in John O'Hanlon, *Life of St. Brigid, Virgin, First Abbess of Kildare, Special Patroness of Kildare Diocese, and General Patroness of Ireland* (Dublin, Joseph Dollard, 1877), for a detailed analysis of the authorship and accuracy of the various lives of Brigid.
17 Condren, *op cit*, p. 56.
18 Rev J.A. Knowles, OSA, *St. Brigid, Patroness of Ireland* (Dublin, Browne and Nolan, 1907), p. 104.
19 Bourke, *op cit*, p. 48.
20 Knowles, *op cit*, p. 154.
21 Alice Curtayne, *St. Brigid of Ireland* (New York, Sheed and Ward, 1954), p. 65.
22 O'Hanlon, *op cit*, p. 51, 52.
23 Caitriona Clarke, *The Story of Saint Brigid* (Dublin, Veritas, 2015), p. 23.
24 Condren, *op cit*, p. 65–66.
25 For example Knowles, Iona, to name but two.
26 McCormack, *op cit*, pp 128–9.
27 Bourke, *op cit*, p. 45.

28 Mary Condren in interview referring to *The Serpent and the Goddess* https://www.threemonkeysonline.com/sexuality-sin-and-sacrifice-deconstructing-the-patriarchy-an-interview-with-dr-mary-condren/2/
29 Sasha Weiss, *Judy Chicago: The Godmother*, New York Times Magazine, 7 February 2018, online https://www.nytimes.com/2018/02/07/t-magazine/judy-chicago-dinner-party.html [Accessed 12/07/2021] and for more on Chicago's Table, see McCormack, *op cit*, p. 190.
30 Diana Leatham, *The Story of St. Brigid of Ireland* (London, The Faith Press, 1955).
31 Image, *Saint Brigid by Seán Branigan, Storyboard Workshop image displayed on* https://www.herstory.ie/brigidsday [Accessed 10/08/2021].
32 Jim Fitzpatrick https://jimfitzpatrick.com/2020/02/01/the-story-of-the-creation-of-brid-2020/ [Accessed 10/08/2021].
33 Courtney Davis, Goddess Collection "Brigid's Fire" https://www.taraonlinestore.com/product-page/gd22-brigid-s-fire [Accessed 10/08/2021].
34 Josephine Hardiman https://www.etsy.com/ie/shop/JosephineHardiman?section_id=24066547 [Accessed 10/08/2021].
35 Re-lit in 1993 by Mary Teresa Cullen, the then leader of the Brigidine Sisters in Solas Bhríde, Brigid's flame was perpetually lit in 2006 in Kildare Town Square from the flame tended in Solas Bhríde. Brigid's sacred flame continues to burn at the top of a beautiful sculpture encased in a bronze acorn cup. See https://solasbhride.ie/new-sculpture-of-st-brigid/ [Accessed 10/08/2021].
36 For more on rituals by wells see https://www.clarelibrary.ie/eolas/coclare/history/saint_brigid_ritual.htm [Accessed 13/08/2021] and for a comprehensive analysis of Hymns and Poems about Brigid see Kissane, Chapter 9.
37 Lily M. O'Brennan, Annotated Typescript Draft of Article 'Naoim Brigid: The Mary of the Gael'. 31 Jan 1948. Ceannt and O'Brennan Papers, 1851–1953. MS 41,505/2/13 National Library of Ireland.
38 Allenwood Middle, Co. Kildare. National Folklore Collection, UCD *Schools' Collection, Volume 0775, Page* 001a Duchas.ie [Accessed 16/09/2021].
39 National Folklore Collection, UCD *Schools' Collection*, Volume 1095 Duchas.ie [Accessed 10/08/2021].
40 National Folklore Collection, UCD *Schools' Collection*, Volume 0126 page 469 Duchas.ie [Accessed 16/09/2021].

41 RTÉ Archives, *A Booklet Produced for the Mother and Child Scheme* 731 x 1024 [Accessed 23/05/2021].
42 McCormack, *op cit*, p.155.
43 O'Brennan, *op cit*. Ceannt and O'Brennan Papers, 1851–1953. MS 41,505/2/13 National Library of Ireland.
44 See Marion Woodman, *The Pregnant Virgin: A Process of Psychological Transformation* (New York, Inner City Books, 1985), for more analysis of the virgin archetype.
45 Condren, interview, *op cit*.
46 Iona, *The Story of Saint Brigid in the Form of a Dialogue Between St. Blath (6th century) and a Novice in One of Saint Brigid's Convents* (Dublin, Talbot Press, 1929), p. 10.
47 Condren, *op cit*, p. 210, quoted in interview with Andrew Lawless.
48 Patrick Logan, *The Holy Wells of Ireland*, quoted in David W. Atherton and Michael P. Peyton, *Saint Brigid: Holy Wells, Patterns and Relics*, p. 2.
49 Curtayne, *op cit*, p. 70.
50 "Brigid's Well". Informant: Brigid Kerrigan, Stranorlar, Co. Donegal, *Schools' Collection*, Volume 1095, Page 132, National Folklore Collection, UCD. Duchas.ie [Accessed 10/08/2021].
51 Rachel Kushner, *The Hard Crowd: Essays 200–2020* (London, Jonathan Cape, 2021), pp 230, 236.
52 See Brian Wright, *Brigid: Goddess, Druidess and Saint* (Stroud, History Press, 2009) p. 227, for an account of the mantle in Bruges, from which this tiny piece was taken. Wright details various examinations (1866, 1935, 1976) which concluded that the mantle was authentic. He does not, however, make any reference to the tiny piece of mantle held in Dublin.
53 Personal email correspondence with Sr. Gabrielle Fox, May 2021.
54 See Chapter 3 of O'Hanlon, *op cit*, for more details on the fifth century rules of dress.
55 https://vatican.com/14/Relics-Reliquary-Of-Saint [Last accessed 11/08/2021]
56 Mary Condren https://www.threemonkeysonline.com/sexuality-sin-and-sacrifice-deconstructing-the-patriarchy-an-interview-with-dr-mary-condren/2/ [Accessed 13/09/2021]

ALL OF THIS WAS WILD

1. Margaret Mac Curtain, *Ariadne's Thread: Writing Women into Irish History* (Galway, Arlen House, 2008), p. 122.
2. Noel Kissane, *Saint Brigid of Kildare: Life, Legend and Cult* (Dublin, Four Courts Press/Open Air, 2017), p. 80.
3. Diana Leatham, *The Story of St. Brigid of Ireland* (London, Faith Press, 1955), p. 18.
4. Rev J.A. Knowles, OSA, *St. Brigid, Patroness of Ireland* (Dublin, Browne and Nolan, 1907), p. 44.
5. *Ibid.*
6. Leatham, *op cit*, p. 29.
7. Kissane, *op cit*, p. 109.
8. *Ibid*, p. 123.
9. See Chapters IX and XIV in John O'Hanlon, *Life of St. Brigid, Virgin, First Abbess of Kildare, Special Patroness of Kildare Diocese, and General Patroness of Ireland* (Dublin, Joseph Dollard, 1877), for a detailed analysis of Kilbrides and wells.
10. Alice Curtayne, *St. Brigid of Ireland* (New York, Sheed and Ward, 1954), p. 4.
11. Nuala Ní Dhomhnaill, *Selected Essays*, edited by Oona Frawley (Dublin, New Island, 2005), p. 160.
12. Second verse of "The Plains of Sweet Kildare" by P. McCormack, Cill Dara, printed in Peadar Mac Suibhne and Patrick McCormack, *Saint Brigid and the Shrines of Kildare* (Naas, Leinster Leader, 1972), p. 37.
13. Mary Condren, *The Serpent and The Goddess* (Dublin, New Island, 2002 [1989]), p. 67
14. Mac Suibhne and McCormack, *op cit*, p. 34.
15. http://searchingforimbas.blogspot.com/p/brigids-wayside-well-kildare.html [Accessed 13/09/2021]
16. https://intokildare.ie/st-brigids-trail/ [Accessed 13/09/2021]
17. Sean Scully interviewed by Lara Marlowe, "I am an Irishman and I love a Good Fight", *Irish Times*, Ticket, Saturday 10 July 2021, p. 62.
18. Kerri Ní Dochartaigh, *Thin Places* (Cannongate, 2021), Kindle Edition, location 708, 712.
19. Margaret Stokes, *Six Months in the Apennines: Or, A Pilgrimage in Search of Vestiges of the Irish Saints in Italy* (London and New York, George Bell & Sons, 1892), p. 15.
20. Ní Dochartaigh, *op cit*, location 2525, 2526.

WHAT REMAINS: THE LIGHT THAT SHINES FROM HISTORY

1 Rev J.A. Knowles, OSA, *St. Brigid, Patroness of Ireland* (Dublin: Browne and Nolan, 1907), pp 18–19.
2 *Ibid*, p. 113.
3 *Ibid*, p. 66.
4 According to Melanie Lynch, founder of HerStory (https://www.herstory.ie/brigidsday [Accessed 10/08/2021]) Brigid "reemerged as a fitting heroine of the Marriage Equality and Repeal the 8th referendums – both extraordinary victories of compassion". It strikes me that to re emerge, there has to be a disappearance or a hiding. What I've found is that even through her Christianised and sanitised symbols (the rushes, the crosses, the rags) she is everywhere. Maybe we need to acknowledge Brigid as a heroine of the female body – for example, Brigid is central to the Woman Spirit Ireland formed by Mary Condren.
5 Catherine McCormack, *Women in the Picture: Women, Art and the Power of Looking* (London, Icon Books, 2021), p. 98, 137.
6 Noel Kissane, *Saint Brigid of Kildare: Life, Legend and Cult* (Dublin: Four Courts Press/Open Air, 2017), p. 103 Kissane discusses the discrepancies around her date of birth and concludes that they might have 'arisen from errors in transcribing the minims in the Roman numerals". He puts the date of birth at 439, death at 524.
7 Marie Heaney, *Over Nine Waves: A Book of Irish Legends* (London, Faber, 1994), p. 235.
8 Brighid's Kiss/Lá Lugh by Gerry O'Connor, Sung by Eithne Ní Uallacháin, English words Féinne O'Connor https://www.youtube.com/watch?v=gTkSqmwQSYk&t=0s [Accessed 17/08/ 2021]
9 Mary Condren, *WATERtea with Mary Condren, "Preparing to Celebrate the Festival of Brigid"* 54:22. YouTube https://www.youtube.com/watch?v=ZYEScCuQ9us [Accessed 17/08/2021].
10 Una O'Hagan interviewed by Deirdre Falvey about *The Book of St. Brigid* by Colm Keane and Una O'Hagan (Capel Island Press) in *The Irish Times* 11/09/2021, p. 17.

PORTAL

About the Author

Shauna Gilligan is a novelist and short story writer living in Kildare. Her writing has been published in journals such as *The Stinging Fly* and *New Welsh Review*. She has a PhD in Creative Writing and teaches in further and higher education. She is particularly interested in exploring the body, the crossover of art and literature in storytelling, the depiction of historical events in fiction, and creative processes. She has received many awards for her writing including the Cecil Day Lewis award from Kildare County Council.

About the Artist

Margo McNulty was born in Achill Island, Co. Mayo, and studied Fine Art in Galway and completed her MFA in NCAD, Dublin. In April 2021, Mayo County Council awarded her a residency with the Jackie Clarke Collection, Ballina. The commission is part of the Decade of Centenaries celebrations. McNulty has exhibited widely over the last few years with solo exhibitions and group shows in Ireland, Sweden, Poland and the UK. She has taken part in a number of Irish and international residencies, and her work resides in major collections nationwide. Her work is influenced by traditions inherent in Irish culture and deals with hidden history, memory and place. The work concerns itself with episodes of chance, the intersection of personal and public histories and how these histories and meanings can be embedded in material objects.
margomcnulty.com